Charles I. (Charles Ira) Bushnell, Ebenezer Fletcher

The Narrative of Ebenezer Fletcher

A Soldier of the Revolution

Charles I. (Charles Ira) Bushnell, Ebenezer Fletcher

The Narrative of Ebenezer Fletcher
A Soldier of the Revolution

ISBN/EAN: 9783337133467

Printed in Europe, USA, Canada, Australia, Japan

Cover: Foto ©ninafisch / pixelio.de

More available books at **www.hansebooks.com**

THE

NARRATIVE

OF

EBENEZER FLETCHER,

A SOLDIER OF THE REVOLUTION,

Written by Himself.

WITH

AN INTRODUCTION AND NOTES,

BY

CHARLES I. BUSHNELL.

NEW YORK:

PRIVATELY PRINTED.

—1866.—

TO

DEXTER FLETCHER,

OF MOUNT VERNON, N. H.,

THE ELDEST SURVIVING SON OF

EBENEZER FLETCHER,

THIS TRACT

IS RESPECTFULLY

DEDICATED.

INTRODUCTION.

EBENEZER FLETCHER, the author of the
following narrative, was the son of John
Fletcher, and was born in New Ipswich, in
the State of New Hampshire, on the fifth day of February,
1761. His mother's maiden name was Elizabeth Foster.
She was the daughter of Abijah Foster, a farmer of New
Ipswich, and one of the first settlers of the place.

After receiving the rudiments of a plain, common school
education, our author, when about fourteen years of age,
was placed under the care of Samuel Cummings, of New
Ipswich, who built and then owned the mills at Mill
Village. He continued with him until the spring of the
year 1777, when he enlisted as a fifer in Capt. Carr's
company, in the battalion commanded by Col. Nathan
Hale, of New Hampshire troops, to serve for the period of

three years. The battalion marched soon after to Ticonderoga, and composed for a while a part of the garrison of that fort ; but on the approach of General Burgoyne, the army evacuated the post, and while on their retreat, were overtaken by the enemy at Hubbardton, where a sharp action took place, in which Mr. Fletcher was severely wounded and taken prisoner. He continued with the British for a few weeks, when, having partially recovered from his wounds, he succeeded in effecting his escape, and after severe trials in the wilderness and among the mountains, without food or company, he at length reached the house of a friend, where he remained a few days, and then returned to his home. On recovering his health, he rejoined his company, and served the remaining part of his term of enlistment, being, in the fall of 1779, in the memorable Indian expedition under the command of General Sullivan, and receiving his discharge from the army on the twentieth day of March of the following year.

On his return from the war, he again entered the service of Mr. Cummings, his former employer, and after remaining with him a while, he at length purchased from him the mills at Mill Village, and carried them on successfully for a number of years. He subsequently engaged in the business of trunk making, which occupation he pursued until within a short period of his decease.

Mr. Fletcher was twice married. His first wife was Miss Polly Cummings, an estimable lady, and the daughter of Mr. Samuel Cummings, before named. She was born in New Ipswich, on the sixteenth of December, 1758, was married in 1786, and died on the twenty-sixth day of February, in the year 1812. By her, Mr. Fletcher had six sons and six daughters. His second wife was Mrs. Mary Foster, widow of Nathaniel Foster, of Ashby, Mass., and daughter of Asa Rendall, whose occupation was that of a farmer. This lady was born in Dunstable, Mass., on the twenty-ninth of December, 1766, became the wife of Mr. Fletcher in the month of June, 1812, and died in Winchendon, Mass., on the twenty-fifth day of January, 1851. By this union, there was no issue.

Mr. Fletcher was short in stature, being but about five feet three inches tall, and proportionably slim, but remarkably active in his movements. He had blue eyes and fair complexion, and his features were small and delicate. He was amiable in his disposition, modest in his deportment, and, though a man of few words, he was cheerful, kind hearted, and a good friend to the poor. Although always sustaining a moral, Christian character, yet he does not seem to have made a public profession of religion until the year 1813. He was then baptised by immersion, and joined the close communion Baptists of his native place.

He was fond of singing, and, at church, he usually sat with
the choir. He was an exemplary professor of religion, and
was noted for his industry, and his strict integrity.

After a life of activity and usefulness, he died in New
Ipswich, on the eighth day of May, 1831, in the 71st year
of his age, in the hope of a blessed immortality. The Rev.
Asaph Merriam, then pastor of the Baptist meeting-house,
preached his funeral sermon, taking his text from the 37th
chap. Psalms, 37th verse—"Mark the perfect *man*, and
behold the upright : for the end of *that* man is peace." The
remains of the deceased, followed by a large number of rela-
tives and friends, were then conveyed to the burial ground
in Mill Village, being the southerly part of the town of
New Ipswich, where they were committed to their kindred
dust. A plain, but neat tombstone, bearing his name, age
and time of decease, marks the spot of his repose.

In conclusion, we would state that the narrative, written
by himself, of his adventures during the Revolutionary war,
was originally published in the year 1813. In 1827 a fourth
edition had appeared. This was reproduced on the 30th
day of January, 1863, in the columns of the " Sentinel,"
a newspaper published in Fitchburg, Massachusetts. The
present issue has been taken from one of the original
imprints of 1827, that being the author's last revised and
most improved edition.

GENERAL FRASER.

NARRATIVE

OF THE

CAPTIVITY & SUFFERINGS

OF

EBENEZER FLETCHER,

OF NEW-IPSWICH,

*Who was severely wounded and taken prisoner at the battle of
Hubbardston, Vt., in the year 1777, by the British and
Indians, at the age of 16 years, after recovering in
part, made his escape from the enemy, and
travelling through a dreary wilderness, followed by wolves, and beset by Tories on
his way, who threatened to take him
back to the enemy, but made his escape from them all, and arrived
safe home.*

——o——

Written by himself, and published at the request of his
friends.

——o——

FOURTH EDITION.
REVISED AND ENLARGED.

——o——

NEW-IPSWICH, N. H.
PRINTED BY S. WILDER,
—1827.—

NARRATIVE.

I EBENEZER FLETCHER, enlisted into the Continental Army, in Capt. Carr's(1) Company,(2) in Col. Nathan Hale's(3) Regiment,(4) as a fifer, and joined the Army at Ticonderoga,(5) under the command of Gen. St. Clair,(6) in the spring of 1777, at which place I was stationed till the retreat of the Army on the 6th of July following.(7)

Early on the morning of the same day, orders came to strike our tents and swing our packs. It was generally conjectured that we were going to battle; but orders came immediately to march.

We marched some distance before light. By sunrise the enemy had landed from their boats, and pursued us so closely as to fire on our rear. A large body of the enemy followed us all day, but kept so far behind as not to be wholly discovered. Their aim was to attack us suddenly next morning, as they did.

Having just recovered from the measles, and not being able to march with the main body, I fell in the rear. The morning after our retreat, orders came very early for the troops to refresh and be ready for marching. Some were eating, some were cooking, and all in a very unfit posture for battle. Just as the sun rose, there was a cry, "*the enemy are upon us.*" Looking round I saw the enemy in line of battle. Orders came to lay down our packs and be ready for action. The fire instantly began. (-) We were but few in number compared to the enemy. At the commencement of the battle, many of our party retreated back into the woods. Capt. Carr came up and says, "My lads advance, we shall beat them yet." A few of us followed him in view of the enemy. Every man was trying to secure himself behind girdled trees, which were standing on the place of action. I made shelter for myself and discharged my piece. Having loaded again and taken aim, my piece missed fire. I brought the same a second time to my face; but before I had time to discharge it, I received a musket ball in the small of my back, and fell with my gun cocked. My uncle, Daniel Foster,* standing but little distance from me, I made out to crawl to him and spoke to him. He and another man lifted me and carried me back some distance and laid me down behind a large tree, where was another man crying out most bitterly with a grievous wound. By this time I had bled so freely, I was very weak and faint. I observed the enemy were like to gain the ground. Our men began to retreat and the enemy to advance. Having no friend to afford me any relief, every one taking care of himself, all things looked very shocking to me; to remain where I was and fall into the hands of the enemy, especially in the condition I was in, expecting to receive no mercy, it came into my mind to conceal myself from them if possible. I made use of

---

* All we know of this person is that he came from Concord, in the county of Merrimac and State of New Hampshire.—*Ed.*

my hands and knees, as well as I could, and crawled
about two rods among some small brush, and got
under a log. Here I lay concealed from the
enemy, who came instantly to the place I lay
wounded at. What became of my distressed part-
ner I know not. The enemy pursued our men in
great haste. Some of them came over the log
where I lay. Some came so near I could almost
touch them. I was not discovered by the enemy
till the battle was over. When they were picking
up the dead and wounded among the brush and
logs, I heard them coming towards me, and began
to be much terrified, lest I should be found. I
flattered myself that our men would come back
after the battle was over and take me off; but to
my great surprise, two of the enemy came so nigh,
I heard one of them say, "Here is one of the
rebels." I lay flat on my face across my hands,
rolled in my blood. I dared not stir, being afraid
they meant me, by saying, "here is one of the
rebels." They soon came to me, and pulled off my
shoes, supposing me to be dead. I looked up and
spoke, telling them I was their prisoner, and begged
to be used well. "Damn you," says one, "you

deserve to be used well, don't you? What's such
a young rebel as you fighting for?" One of these
men was an officer, who appeared to be a pretty
sort of a man. He spoke to the soldier, who had
taken my shoes, and says, "Give back the shoes
and help the man into camp." My shoes were
given back by the soldier according to order. The
soldier then raised me upon my feet, and conducted
me to the British camp. Here I found a number
of my brother soldiers in the same situation as
myself. I was laid on the ground and remained in
this posture till the afternoon, before my wound
was dressed. Two Doctors came to my assistance.
They raised me up, and examined my back. One
of them said, "My lad, you stood a narrow chance;
had the ball gone in or out half its bigness, you
must have been killed instantly." I asked him if
he thought there was any prospect of my getting
well again. He answered, "There is some prospect." I concluded by his reply, he considered my
case hazardous. The Doctors appeared to be very
kind and faithful. They pulled several pieces of my
clothes from my wound, which were forced in by
the ball I received.

Some of the enemy were very kind ; while others were very spiteful and malicious. One of them came and took my silver shoe-buckles and left me an old pair of brass ones, and said *exchange was no robbery;* but I thought it robbery at a high rate. Another came and took off my neck handkerchief. An old negro came and took my fife, which I considered as the greatest insult I had received while with the enemy. The Indians often came and abused me with their language; calling us Yankees and rebels; but they were not allowed to injure us. I was stripped of everything valuable about me.

The enemy soon marched back to Ticonderoga, and left only a few to take care of the wounded. I was treated as well as I could expect. Doctor Haze was the head Doctor, and he took true care that the prisoners were well treated. Doctor Blocksom, an under surgeon, appeared to be very kind indeed : he was the one who had the care of me : he never gave me any insulting or abusive language; he sometimes would say, " Well, my lad, think you'll be willing to list in the King's service, if you should get well?" My answer was always *no*. The officers would flatter me to list in their service; telling me they were very sure to conquer the country, since they had got our strongest post. I told them I should not list.

But among all the troubles I met with, I received particular favors from two of the British. This conduct appeared to me very remarkable; why or wherefore it should be I knew not; but He who hath the hearts of all men in his hands, gave me favor in their sight. They would often visit me, and asked me if I wanted anything to eat or drink. If I did, I had it. The first time one of these friends came to me, was soon after I was brought to the camp.

As I lay on the ground, he asked me if I did not want a bed to lie on: I told him I did: he went and got a large hemlock bark, and finding many old coats and overalls, taken from the dead and wounded, he put them in the bark, made me a bed, and laid me into it. He built a shelter over me with barks, to keep the rain from me, which was a great kindness, as it rained exceeding hard the next night. He went to a spring, and brought me water as often as I wanted, which was very often, being very dry: my loss of blood occasioning much thirst. He asked me, also, if I wanted to eat. I answered yes: for having eat but little that day, I was very faint and hungry. He told me he did not know as it was in his power to procure anything for me, but would go and try. After an absence of considerable time (certainly the time seemed long) he returned with a piece of broiled pork and broiled liver, telling me this was all the food he could get: I thanked him, and told him it was very good.

The next day he came and told me he had orders to march, and must therefore leave me: was very sorry he could stay no longer with me, but hoped somebody would take care of me; taking me by the hand he wished me well and left me.

The loss of so good a friend grieved me exceedingly; but I soon heard that my other friend was ordered to stay behind to help take care of the wounded. My spirits, which before were very much depressed, when I heard of this, were much exhilarated; and once more I felt tolerably happy. The difference in mankind never struck me more sensibly than while a prisoner. Some would do everything in their power to make me comfortable and cheerful; while others abused me with the vilest of language; telling me that the prisoners would all be hanged; that they would drive all the damned rebels into the sea, and that their next winter quarters would be in Boston. They certainly wintered in Boston; but to their great disappointment and chagrin, as *prisoners of war*.

But to return. My wound being now a little better, I began to think of escaping from the enemy. Two of my fellow-prisoners agreed to accompany me; one of them being well acquainted with the way to Otter Creek.(5) This plan, however, failed; for before we had an opportunity for making our escape, Doctor Haze called upon my companions to be ready to march for Ticonderoga: telling them that the next morning they must leave this place. Thus I found, that as soon as the prisoners were able to ride, they were ordered to Ticonderoga. Being thus disappointed I begged of the Doctor to let me go with them. Says he, " You are very dangerously wounded, and it is improper for you to ride so far yet; but as soon as you are able you shall go." Being thus defeated I

again resolved to run away, even if I went alone,
and it was not long before I had an opportunity.
As all the prisoners were sent off except such
as were badly wounded, they thought it unneces-
sary to guard us very closely. I soon was able to
go to the spring, which was at a little distance
from the camp. Thither I often went for water for
myself and the Hessians, (*) who, by the way,
appeared to be pleased with me. I often waited
upon them, brought them water, made their beds,
&c., and found my fare the better for it. I often
walked out into the woods where the battle was
fought; went to the tree where I was shot down,
observed the trees which were very much marked
with the balls. Looking around one day, I found
some leaves of a Bible; these I carried into the
camp, and diverted myself by reading them; for I
felt much more contented when I had something
to read. My friend, whom I have before mentioned, one day brought me a very good book,
which he told me to keep as a present from him.
This I heartily thanked him for, and whenever
I was tired by walking would lay down and
read.

On the 22d of July, a number of men came down from Ticonderoga, with horses and litters sufficient to carry off the remainder of the wounded. Doctor Haze came to us and told us, that to-morrow we should all be carried where we should have better care taken of us. Says he, "I will send the orderly sergeant, who will see that your bloody clothes are well washed." This he thought would be very agreeable news to us. I pretended to be very much pleased, though I was determined never to go. I told the person who lay next to me that I intended to run away; desired him to make them believe I had taken the north road, if they inclined to pursue me, for I should take the south. Says he, "I will do all in my power to assist you, and wish it was possible for me to go with you."

I made it my business that day to procure provisions sufficient for my journey. I had spared a little bread from my daily allowance, and although dry and mouldy, yet it was the best to be had. I had a large jack-knife left of which the enemy had not robbed me; I sold this for a pint of wine, thinking it would do me more good on my march than the knife, as the event proved. The wine I put in a bottle, and carefully stowed it in my pocket. I was hard put to it to get my shirt washed and dried before evening. However, agreeing with some to make their beds if they would dry my shirt, it was ready to put on by dark. I then went to my tent, took off my coat and jacket, and put on my clean shirt over my dirty one, and having filled my pockets with the little provision I had saved, I began to march homeward shoeless; reflecting what I should do for so material a part of my clothing. It came into my mind that one Jonathan Lambart had died of his wounds a day or two before and left a good pair of shoes. Supposing my right to them equal to any other person, I took them and put them on.

It being dark, I went out undiscovered, and steered into the woods. After going a little way, I turned into the road and made a halt. Now was the trying scene! The night being very dark, everything before me appeared gloomy and discouraging; my wound was far from being healed; my strength much reduced by the loss of blood, pain and poor living; thus situated, to travel alone, I knew not where, having no knowledge of the way,

I thought would be highly presumptuous. How far I should have to travel before I could reach any inhabitants, I could not tell: Indians, I supposed, were lurking about, and probably I might be beset by them and murdered or carried back: and if I avoided them, perhaps I might perish in the wilderness.

Reflecting upon these things, my resolution began to flag, and I thought it most prudent to return and take my fate. I turned about and went back a few rods, when the following words struck me as if whispered in my ear: *Put not your hands to the plough and look back.* I immediately turned about again, fully resolved to pursue my journey through the woods; but before morning, had I been possessed of millions of gold, I would freely have given the whole to have been once more with the enemy. The road which I had to travel, was newly opened, leading from Hubbardston (n) to Otter-Creek. The night being dark and the road very crooked, I found it very difficult to keep it; often running against trees and rocks, before I knew I was out of it; and then it was with much trouble that I found it again, which sometimes I was obliged to do upon my hands and knees, and often up to my knees in mire.

About 12 o'clock I heard something coming towards me; what it could be I knew not. I halted and looked back; it was so dark I was at a loss to determine what it was: but thought it looked like a dog. That a dog should be so far from inhabitants, I thought very strange. I at once concluded that he belonged to the Indians, and that they were not far off. I however ventured to speak to him, and he immediately came to me; I gave him a piece of mouldy bread, which he eat and soon appeared fond of me. At first I was afraid he would betray me to the Indians; but soon found him of service; for I had not gone far before I heard the noise of some wild beast. I had just set down to rest me, with my back against a tree, my wound being very painful. As the beast approached, my dog appeared very much frighted; laid close down by me and trembled, as if he expected to be torn in pieces. I now began to be much terrified; I however set very still, knowing it would do no good to run. He came within two rods of me, and stopped. I was unable to deter-

mine what it was, but supposed it was a wolf. I
soon found I was not mistaken. After looking at
me some time, he turned about and went off; but
before long returned with a large reinforcement.
In his absence I exerted myself to the utmost to
get forward, fearing he would be after me again.
After travelling about half an hour, I was alarmed
with the most horrible howling, which I supposed
to be near the tree which I rested by. Judge what
my feelings were, when I found these beasts of prey
were pursuing me, and expected every minute to
be devoured by them. But in the midst of this
trouble, to my infinite joy, I discovered fires but a
little way before me, which, from several circumstances, I was sure were not built by Indians; I
therefore at once concluded they were fires of some
scouting party of Americans, and I made great
haste to get to them, lest I should be overtaken by
the wolves, which were now but a little behind. I
approached so near the fires as to hear men talk,
when I immediately discovered them to be enemies.
Thus disappointed I knew not what course to take;
if I continued in the woods, I should be devoured
by wild beasts; for having eat of the bodies which

were left on the field of battle, they continued
lurking for more. If I gave myself up to the
enemy, I should certainly be carried back to Ticen-
deroga, and to Canada, and probably fare no better
for attempting to run away. Which way to escape
I knew not; I turned a little out of the path and
lay down on the ground to hear what was said by
the enemy, expecting every moment they would
discover me: the darkness of the night, however,
prevented. These howling beasts approached as
near the fires as they dared, when they halted and
continued their horrid yell for some time, being
afraid to come so nigh as I was. After the howling
had ceased, I began to think of getting round the
enemy's camp; being pretty certain that, as yet, I
was not discovered. I arose from the ground and
took a course, which I thought would carry me
round the enemy's camp. After travelling a little
way, I came to the foot of a high mountain; to go
round it I thought would carry me too much out of
my course; I resolved therefore to ascend it; with
much difficulty I arrived at the top, then took a tack
to the right; travelling that course some time I
found I was bewildered and lost, and which way to

go to find the road again I knew not, having neither
moon nor stars to direct me; so I wandered about
in this wilderness till almost day, when I became so
fatigued and worried, that I was obliged to lay
down again. Judge what a person's feelings must
be in such a situation.

I now repented of my ever leaving the enemy.
Here I was lost in the woods, with but very little
provision, my wounds extremely painful, and little
or no prospect of ever seeing human beings again.
Thus I lay and reflected, my dog walking round me
like a faithful sentinel, till I fell asleep; but was
soon alarmed with the noise of cannon, which I
concluded by the direction must be at Ticonderoga.
Never was sound more grateful to my ears than
this cannon. I thought I might possibly live to
reach the place, and though an enemy's camp,
I would have given anything to be with them
again.

Soon after the morning gun was fired, I heard
the drums beat in the camp which I had visited in
the night: this noise was still more grateful, for I
was sure they were not at a great distance. With
much difficulty I got upon my legs again, with

a determination to go to their camp. I found, however, that I could scarcely stand; for having laid down when I was very sweaty, I had taken cold, and was so stiff and sore, that I could hardly move. I now had recourse to my little bottle of wine, which relieved me very much, and then began to march towards the drums, which still continued beating.

After travelling a little way, I heard a cock crow, which appeared near the drums. I thought it of little consequence which object to pursue, both being nearly in the same direction. But the noise of the drums soon ceased, and I steered for the other object, which soon brought me into open land and in sight of a house. I got to the door just as the man arose from his bed. After the usual compliments, I asked him how far it was to the British encampments? He answered about fifty rods. " Do you want to go to them?" says he. I never was more at a stand what reply to make. As none of the enemy appeared about the house, I thought if I could persuade this man to befriend me, I possibly might avoid them; but if he should prove to be a tory, and know from whence I came, he

would certainly betray me. I stood perhaps a
minute without saying a word. He seeing my confusion, spoke again to me: "Come," said he, "come
into the house." I went in and sat down. I will
tell you, said I, what I want, if you will promise
not to hurt me. He replied, "I will not injure
you, if you do not injure us." This answer did not
satisfy me, for as yet I could not tell whether he
would be a friend or foe. I sat and viewed him
for some minutes, and at last resolved to tell him
from whence I came and where I wished to go, let
the event be what it would. I was a soldier, said
I, in the Continental army, was dangerously wounded
and taken prisoner, had made my escape from the
enemy, and after much fatigue and peril, had got
through the woods, being directed to this house by
the crowing of a cock. He smiled and said, "You
have been rightly directed, for had you gone to
either of my neighbors, you undoubtedly would
have been carried to the enemy again; you have
now found a friend, who will if possible protect
you. It is true they have forced me to take the
oath of allegiance to the king; but I sincerely hope
the Americans will finally prevail, for I believe

their cause to be just and equitable; should they
know of my harboring rebels, as they call us, I
certainly should suffer for it. Anything I can do
for you without exposing my own life, I will do."
I thanked him for his kindness, and desired him not
to expose himself on my account.

After giving me something to eat and drink, he
concealed me in a chamber, where he said I might
stay till the dew was off and then go out into some
secret place in the bushes, there to continue till
night: this he said was necessary, as the enemy
were often plundering about his house, and if I continued in it, I should probably be discovered,
which would ruin him. A little boy was set as a
sentinel at the door, who was to give notice if the
enemy came near. I had not been in the house
half an hour, before a number of them came in, but
with no other design than to buy some rum and
milk, and to borrow a pot for cooking.

As soon as they were gone, the woman came into
the chamber to dress my wound. She washed it
with rum, applied dressings, and bound it up as
well as she could. She showed every mark of kindness to me, but her husband, whose name was

Moulton, in a day or two after I got to his house, was pressed by the enemy to bring stores from Skeensborough* (12) with his team, and I never saw the good old man any more. His wife was in much trouble, lest the enemy should find me in the house and be so enraged as to kill all the family. She permitted her little boy to guide me to the bushes, where I might secrete myself: she gave me a blanket to lie on. The boy went with me to my lurking place, that I might be easily found, so as to receive refreshment. When night came on, I was called by the boy to the house again, and took my old stand in the chamber; the woman feared I should receive injury by lodging out of doors. She informed me that a man would lodge there that night, who was brother-in-law to her husband; and who had actually taken up arms against his country. I told her I apprehended danger from tarrying in the house; she said there would not be any; I then lay snug in my straw.

In a short time the tory came for some drink; the indiscreet woman told him she had an American

---

* In Washington County, in the State of New York. It is now known as White Hall.—*Ed.*

in the chamber, who had been taken prisoner by
the British and had escaped. He asked her what
kind of a man I was. She told him I was a young
fellow and wanted much to get home, and begged
that I might not be taken back to the enemy or
betrayed. His answer was very rough, and I began
to think I was gone for it. I expected to be forced
back; but the woman interceding so hard for me,
softened the ferocity of my tory enemy. Knowing
I was discovered, I crawled from my hiding place,
and began a conversation with the man. He asked
me if I belonged to the rebel service? I told him I
belonged to the Continental service. "What is that,"
says he, "but the rebel service?" He addressed
me in very insolent language, and said he was
very sorry to have me leave the king's troops in the
manner I had done, and he would have me to
know I was in his hands. I was patient and mild
in my situation, telling him I was at his disposal.
My good mistress often put in a word on my
behalf.

After some time spent in this way, the man
asked me if he should chance to be taken, and in
my power as I was in his, whether I should let him

escape? I told him I should. "Then," says he,
" if you will promise this, I will not detain you ;
also, that if you are retaken before you reach home,
you will not inform, that you have seen me, or have
been at my brother's." I gave him my promise.
His advice to me was immediately to set out, for
if I should stay long I might be picked up by some
person. " And," says he, " I advise you to travel
in the night, and hide in the day, for many volunteers are reconnoitering up and down the country."
I concluded to travel ; but my feeling landlady
thought it best to stay a few days longer. My
friend tory said it was best for me to travel as soon
as possible. " If you are determined to go to-night,"
said the woman, " I will dress your wound and give
you food for your journey." I told her I would go
as soon as possible. She then dressed my wound
for the last time, and filled my pockets with good
provision. After thanking her for her kindness, it
being all the compensation I could make, and I
believe all that she desired, I left her.

But before I proceed on my journey, I must tell
you, that my dog, who had accompanied me
through many dangers, I was obliged to drive from

me ; when in the chamber, he would commonly lay
at the foot of the stairs. Mrs. Moulton often told
me, she was afraid he would betray me, for as the
enemy were often in, should they see the dog,
might suspect that somebody was in the chamber.
I told her, with much regret, to drive him away ;
she with her little boy tried all in their power to
get rid of him, but in vain ; the dog would stay
about the house ; at length she called me to drive
him away ; I came down, and after much difficulty,
effected it.

But to return. After being told the course I
must take, I began my journey in the night, which
was dark and cloudy, through the woods. I had
not travelled more than two hours, before I got lost.
I concluded I had missed the road, and having
reached the end of one I was then in, began to
think of going back. My wound began to be very
painful, and I was so sore, I could scarcely go.
While I was seeking for the road again, there came
up a thunder shower, and rained fast. I crawled
into an old forsaken hovel, which was near, and lay
till the shower was over ; then went back half a
mile and found the road once more. The road

being newly opened through the woods was very bad, and it was with much difficulty I could get along, often tumbling over roots and stones, and sometimes up to my knees in mire. I once fell and was obliged to lay several minutes, before I could recover myself.

About 12 o'clock at night, as I was walking in this wilderness, I was surprised by two large wild animals, which lay close by the road, and started up as soon as they saw me; ran a few rods and turned about towards me; whether they were bears or wolves, I could not tell; I was, however, exceedingly terrified, and would have given any thing for my dog again. One of them followed me for a long time; sometimes would come close to me, and at others, kept at a considerable distance. At last he got discouraged and left me, and certainly I did not regret his absence.

At daylight, I came to open land, and discovered a house belonging to Col. Mead. I was not a little rejoiced to see his house, as I knew he would be a friend to me; but my joy was of short continuance, for as soon as I looked into the door, I saw marks of the enemy; every thing belonging to the house being carried off or destroyed. I thought it not prudent to go into the house lest some of the enemy might be within; so I passed on as fast as possible; it now began to grow light; and what to do with myself I could not tell. My friends had advised me to lay concealed in the day time and travel in the night.

When I viewed the depredations the enemy had made on the inhabitants, and many of whom had fled; not knowing how far I must travel to find friends, and my wound being very troublesome, I reflected long, whether to tarry and be made prisoner, or push forward through a dreary wilderness; death seemed to threaten me on all sides: however, I collected resolution sufficient to make to the east; I conceived myself exposed by my uniform and bloody clothes; to prevent a discovery by any who should be an enemy, I took off my shirt and put it over my coat, by which my uniform was covered; in this line I marched; it being the orders of the British for all tories, who came to join them, to appear in this dress, I considered myself protected.

I travelled till the middle of the day, before

I saw any person; I then met a man driving cattle, as I supposed, to the enemy. He examined me closely, and enquired if I was furnished with a pass. I gave him plausible answers to all his questions, and so far satisfied him as to proceed unmolested. I enquired of him, if he knew one Joshua Priest: he told me he did, and very readily directed me to the place where he lived. Leaving this man, I had not travelled far, before I met a number more, armed; being within about fifty rods of them, I thought to hide myself, but found I could not; I then made towards them, without any apparent fear. Coming up to them, I expected a strict examination; but they only asked me how far it was to such a town: I informed them as well as I could, and pushed on my way.

Being within a mile and a half of said Priest's, I saw two men making towards me; they came to a fence and stopped; I heard them say, "Let's examine this fellow, and know what his business is." One of them asked me where I was going. I told him to Joshua Priest's; he asked me my business there: I answered him upon no bad errand: He says you are a spy: I told him I was

no spy. I did not like the fellow's looks, therefore
dropped the conversation with him, believing he
was one of the enemy. I resolved not to converse
with any one, till I had arrived at Priest's, unless
compelled to. Being almost overcome with fatigue,
I wished for rest; however, these men seemed
determined to stop me or do me some mischief, for
when I walked on, they followed me upon the run,
and in great rage told me, I should go no further,
until I had made known to them who and what I
was; saying, they had asked me a civil question,
and they required a civil answer. I told them
if they would go to Priest's, I would tell them all
the truth and satisfy them entirely; repeating to
them I was no spy. They said they did not mean
to leave me till they were satisfied respecting me.
I then, in short, told them what I had before in
the whole, and added, that I was well acquainted
with Priest, and intended to tarry with him some
time.

We all arrived at Priest's, who at first did not
recollect me. After some pause, he told me he was
surprised to see me, as my father (13) had informed
him I was slain at Hubbardston. I told him, I was

yet alive : but had received a bad wound. His family soon dressed my wound and made me comfortable.

I then in the presence and hearing of my tory followers, told Priest the story of my captivity and escape : also repeated the insolent language used by the tories towards our people, when prisoners with the enemy, finding Priest my friend, I said many severe things against the tories, and fixed my countenance sternly on those fellows, who had pretended to lord it over me and stop me on the way. They bore all without saying a word, but looked as *surly as bulls.*

I soon found these tory gentry had premeditated carrying me back, and were seeking help to prosecute their design. My friend Priest loaded his gun, and said he would give them a grist, if they dared come after me : but failing of getting any persons to join them, I was not molested.

I could often hear my tory followers' threatenings against me, to take me back, saying, I should be able to fight again, and do injury to the enemy. I feared these tories would do hurt, but my fears were quieted by finding the neighbors were my friends, and would afford me their protection. But I will write one more tory plan.

After being at Priest's about ten days, there came, one morning, a number of persons to see me, and appeared very friendly and much concerned, lest I should be taken by the enemy. They informed me a man had arrived from Burgoyne's army, and a party of Indians was to be sent forward to guard the town where I was, and protect the tories and their property; our people coming twice while I was at Priest's to take tory property. These people told me an honest story, and advised me to travel immediately. Being desirous to get home, I told my friend Priest I would not stay any longer. He says, " Don't be scared, I apprehend no danger from the Indians, tarry yet awhile, for your wound is not healed; you are not able to travel through the woods: but do as you think best." These men cried out, " Escape, escape, for your life: Indians will be upon you before to-morrow night."

Having resolved to go on, my friends furnished me with provision sufficient for my journey. Without doubts or fears I went on my way, and after travelling all day I arrived at a place called Ludlow. (๑) From this town the people all fled and left their habitations. Great was my disappointment! I spent the night in a melancholy manner: having neither fire nor bed to comfort my shivering and impaired body.

About day, I set out from the dreary house, which had sheltered me in the night. By travelling, I found I had taken cold, and my wound was very painful. Desponding, I thought it best to go back about seven miles to some inhabitants, rather than to proceed homeward. Just before night I arrived at the place of the inhabitants, seven miles back, who received me kindly, and took special care of my wound.

Just before sunset of the third day, after my departure, I came to my old friend Priest's again, who appeared very glad to see me. Now it was not any friendship in my tory visitors, who advised me to escape, but for fear I should betray them, their reports afterwards proving a lie.

At my old friend's, I remained six weeks: in the mean time my wound was almost healed. I was hospitably entertained by him.

Having heard that one Mr. Atwell, belonging to New-Marlborough, (15) was in the neighborhood with a team to move a family, I agreed with him for a horse to ride. After a journey of a few days, I safely arrived at New-Ipswich, (16) and once more participated the pleasure of seeing and enjoying my friends, and *no enemy to make me afraid.*

Not long afterwards, an officer from the army hearing of my return ordered me to be arrested and returned to the main body of the American army, although my wound was scarcely healed. In a few weeks, I joined my corps, then stationed in Pennsylvania; having yet two years to serve my country in the tented field.

We afterwards went on an expedition against the Indians, to the Genesee Country, a long and tedious march, commanded by Gen. Sullivan, (17) where we drove the savages before us, burnt their huts, destroyed their corn. (18) The first Indian settlement we came to was called Tiauger, (19) where they lay in ambush, in a thick wood, on a hill, where they fired on our men and killed seven; after that we were ordered to march in the following order: the army was divided into four columns, and the head of each column had a horn or trumpet, and each of these divisions marched as far apart as they could hear each other sound: we marched in this line all the way afterward, if we had not they undoubtedly would have waylaid and killed us all. There were two men that left their place and went out from the main body and were taken by the Indians, and tortured to death in the most cruel manner. (20)

Our provision was like to fail: we had to go on half allowance a long time, or we should have starved. Finding few enemies to contend with in that quarter, as they were not disposed to meet us in the open field, we received the gladly obeyed orders to return to New-England, where we remained the ensuing autumn. Nothing more of importance, to me or the reader, occurred, until the three long years rolled away, except when in Pennsylvania, I had the honor of being acquainted with Gen. Washington (21) and Gen. Lafayette,(22) and then I received my discharge.*

And now, kind reader, wishing that you may

---

* He received his discharge March 20, 1780.—*Ed.*

forever remain ignorant of the real sufferings of the veteran soldier, from hunger and cold, from sickness and captivity, I bid you a cordial adieu.

EBENEZER FLETCHER.(23)

New-Ipswich, Jan., 1813.

NOTES.

(1) CAPT. JAMES CARR was a resident of Somersworth, Strafford Co., N. H. He was Captain of the third company in the second of three battalions raised in New Hampshire in 1776. He eventually attained the rank of Major, and died on the eleventh day of March, 1829.

(2) The following were the officers of the company :

JAMES CARR............of Somersworth. *Captain.*
SAMUEL CHERRY........ " Londonderry.. *First-Lieutenant.*
PELETIAH WHITTEMORE.. " New Ipswich.. *Second-Lieutenant.*
GEORGE FROST .... " Greenland.... *Ensign.*

(3) COL. NATHAN HALE was born in Hampstead. Rockingham Co., N. H., on the 23d day of September, 1743. His mother's maiden name was Elizabeth Wheeler. His father, Moses Hale. was born in Rowley, Mass., in 1703, and died in Rindge, N. H., on the 19th day of June, 1762.

Col. Hale was by occupation a merchant. He came to
Rindge in company with his brothers, Moses and Enoch,
shortly after the first settlement of the place. On the 28th day
of January, 1766, he was married to Abigail Grout, who was
born in Lunenburgh, Mass., March 23d, 1745. This lady was
the daughter of John Grout, who was born in Sudbury, Mass.,
October 14, 1704. Mr. Grout was originally a farmer, but,
during the latter years of his life, followed the profession of
the law. He resided in Lunenburgh a while; thence moved
to Rindge, and subsequently to Jaffrey, N. H., where he died.

Col. Hale commanded the second of three battalions which
were raised in New Hampshire in 1776, to serve for the period
of three years. He was engaged in the battle of Hubbardton,
and was taken prisoner there by the British. Immediately
after the battle, reports, censuring his conduct in that engagement, were circulated, but whether they were well founded,
or originated, as many have supposed, in the envy of some of
his inferior officers, it is difficult now to decide. It is known
that he and his men were at the time of the engagement in a
feeble state of health, and were consequently unfit for military
service. The historians of the day, moreover, attach no
blame to his conduct; and his character, in other respects,
appears to have been irreproachable. Col. Hale, it is said, on
hearing of the reports, wrote to General Washington, request-
ing that he might be exchanged, and thus have the opportunity of vindicating his character by a court-martial, but
before this could be effected, he died, while a prisoner on

Long Island, in the month of September, 1780, he being then thirty-seven years of age. He left, surviving him, his widow, four sons and two daughters, all of whom are now deceased.

Mrs. Hale was a woman of great resolution, and managed her affairs with remarkable success. She lived in Rindge for many years, and died in Chelsea, Vt., on the 14th day of September, 1838, in the ninety-fourth year of her age.

The following are the names of Col. Hale's children, and the times of their birth and death :

1. CHARLOTTE (Mrs. Lowe)..Born Dec. 30, 1766..Died May 5, 1841.
2. THOMAS.................. " Sept. 6. 1769.. " Dec. 1, 1797.
3. NATHAN.... .... " July 1, 1771.. " Jan. 9, 1849.
4. A SON.................. " July 1773.. " Same day.
5. ELIPHALET.............. " May 16. 1775.. " Sept. 26, 1852.
6. POLLY .... " April 26, 1778.. " Sept. 26, 1795.
7. HARRY................. " Feb. 10. 1780.. " June 2, 1861.

(4) The following were the officers of the Second Battalion :

NATHAN HALE.... .....of Rindge......... Colonel.
WINBORN ADAMS........ " Durham....... Lieutenant-Col.
BENJAMIN TITCOMB...... " Dover......... Major.
WILLIAM ELLIOT........ " Exeter......... Adjutant.
JERRY FOGG .... " Kensington ..... Paymaster.
RICHARD BROWN........ " Unity......... Quarter-Master.
WILLIAM PARKER, JR.... " Exeter......... Surgeon.
PELETIAH WARREN...... " Berwick....... Surgeon's Mate.
AUGUSTUS HIBBARD ..... " Claremont...... Chaplain.

(6) TICONDEROGA—a post-town of Essex County, New-York, on the west side of the south end of Lake Champlain, and at

the north end of Lake George, twelve miles south of Crown Point, and ninety-five miles north of Albany. In 1860 the population of the town was 2,270.

Ticonderoga Fort, so famous in American history, was erected on an eminence on the north side of a peninsula of about five hundred acres, elevated upwards of one hundred feet above Lake Champlain, at the mouth of Lake George's outlet. Considerable remains of the fortifications are still to be seen. The stone walls of the fort, which are still standing, are in some places thirty feet high. The fort was built by the French in 1756, and was called by them "*Carillon*," a word signifying a jingling racket or clatter. By the Indians it was known by the Iroquois name "*Cheeonderoga*," signifying "sounding waters." It had all the advantages that art or nature could give it, being defended on three sides by water surrounded by rocks, and on half of the fourth by a swamp, and where that fails, the French erected a breast work nine feet high. The British and Colonial troops, under General Abercrombie, were defeated here in the year 1758, but the place was taken the year following by General Amherst. Ticonderoga was the first fortress attacked by the Americans in the Revolutionary war. It was surprised by Cols. Ethan Allen and Benedict Arnold, on the 10th day of May, 1775; was re-taken by General Burgoyne on the 6th day of July, 1777; and was evacuated after his surrender, the garrison returning to St. Johns.

Mount Defiance lies about a mile south of the fort, and Mount Independence is about half a mile distant, on the opposite side of the lake, in Addison County, Vermont.

(ₐ) Major-General Arthur St. Clair was born in Edinburgh, Scotland, in the year 1734. He came to America with Admiral Boscawen in 1755. In 1759 and 1760 he served in Canada as a Lieutenant, under Gen. Wolfe, and after the peace of 1763, was appointed to the command of Fort Ligonier, in Pennsylvania. Here he settled, and becoming a citizen of Pennsylvania, was appointed to several offices of a civil nature. When the Revolution commenced, he embraced the cause of the Americans, and in January, 1776, was appointed to command a battalion of Pennsylvania militia. He was engaged in the expedition to Canada, and was the second in command in the proposed attack on the British post at Trois Rivières. He was soon after ordered to join the army in New Jersey, and was engaged in the battles of Trenton and Princeton. On the ninth day of August, 1776, he was appointed a Brigadier-General, and in the month of February following, was made a Major-General. He was the commanding officer at Ticonderoga when that post was invested by the British, and having a garrison of but about 2,000 men, badly equipped, and very short of ammunition and stores, he was compelled to evacuate it, which he did on the 6th day of July, 1777. Charges of cowardice, treachery and incapacity were brought against him for this step, but a court of inquiry honorably acquitted him. In 1780 he was ordered to Rhode Island, but circumstances prevented him from going thither. When the allied armies marched towards Virginia in 1781, to attack Cornwallis, Gen. St. Clair was directed to remain at Philadelphia with the recruits of the Pennsylvania line for the protection of Congress. He was, however, soon allowed to join the army, and reached Yorktown during the siege. From Yorktown he was sent with a considerable force to join Gen. Greene, which he did near Savannah, Georgia, and at the conclusion of the war, he returned to his former residence in Pennsylvania. In 1783 he was a member of the Council of Censors of Pennsylvania, and the same year was elected President of the Cincinnati Society of that State. In 1786 he was elected a delegate to Congress, and in February, 1787, was chosen President of that body. In 1788 he was appointed Governor of the territory of the United States north-west of the Ohio, which office he retained until November, 1802, when he was removed by Mr. Jefferson in consequence of the too free expression of his political opinions. In 1791 he commanded an army employed against the Miami Indians, and was defeated on the 4th of November, with the loss of between six hundred to seven hundred men. On this occasion a portion of the citizens were loud in their censures of his conduct; but a committee of the House of Representatives, appointed to examine into the cause of the failure of the expedition, upon hearing his defense, honorably exculpated him from blame. In the following year he resigned his

commission as Major-General, and in his old age, being
reduced to poverty, and embarrassed by debts, he applied to
Congress for relief, but his claims on the sympathy of his
country were listened to with indifference, and admitted with
reluctance. In the year 1817, after a great suspense, he
obtained a pension of sixty dollars a month, which he did not,
however, live long to enjoy. He died at Laurel Hill, near
Phil., on the 31st day of August, 1818, at the age of eighty-
four years. His remains were interred in the Presbyterian
church-yard in Greensburg, Westmoreland Co., Pa., and in 1832
the Masonic fraternity placed a neat monument over his grave.

(7) "Although every possible exertion had been made by Gen.
St. Clair and his men, the state of the American works and
of the garrison was not such as to insure a long and vigorous
defence. The old French fort had been strengthened by
some additional works, several block-houses had been erected,
and some new batteries had been constructed on the side
towards Lake George. The Americans had also fortified a
high circular hill on the east side of the lake opposite to
Ticonderoga, to which they had given the name of Mount
Independence. These two posts were connected by a floating-
bridge twelve feet wide and one thousand feet long, which
was supported by twenty-two sunken piers of large. timber.
This bridge was to have been defended by a boom strongly
fastened together by bolts and chains; but this boom was not
completed when Gen. Burgoyne advanced against the works.

"Notwithstanding the apparent strength of the posts occupied by the Americans, their works were all effectually overlooked and commanded by a neighboring eminence called Sugar Loaf Hill, or Mount Defiance. This circumstance was well known to the American officers, and they had a consultation for the express purpose of considering the propriety of fortifying this mountain; but it was declined, because they believed the British would not think it practicable to plant cannon upon it, and because their works were already so extensive, that they could not be properly manned, the whole garrison consisting of only 2,546 continental troops, and 900 militia; the latter very badly armed and equipped.

"Gen. St. Clair was sensible that he could not sustain a regular siege; still he hoped that the confidence of Burgoyne would induce him to attempt to carry the American works by assault, against which he was resolved to defend himself to the last extremity. But to the surprise and consternation of the Americans, on the 5th of July, the enemy appeared upon Mount Defiance, and immediately commenced the construction of a battery. This battery, when completed, would effectually command all the American works on both sides of the lake, and the line of communication between them; and, as there was no prospect of being able to dislodge the enemy from this post, a council of war was called, by which it was unanimously agreed that a retreat should be attempted that very night, as the only means of saving the army.

" Accordingly, about two o'clock in the morning of the 6th of July, Gen. St. Clair, with the garrison, left Ticonderoga, and at about three o'clock the troops on Mount Independence were put in motion. The baggage, provisions and stores were, as far as practicable, embarked on board 200 batteaux, and despatched, under convoy of five armed gallies, to Skenesborough, while the main body of the army proceeded by land on the route through Hubbardton and Castleton. These affairs were conducted with secrecy and silence, and unobserved by the enemy, till a French officer, imprudently and contrary to orders, set fire to his house. The flames immediately illuminated the whole of Mount Independence, and revealed to the enemy at once the movements and designs of the Americans. It at the same time impressed the Americans with such an idea of discovery and danger, as to throw them into the utmost disorder and confusion.

" About four o'clock, the rear-guard of the Americans left Mount Independence, and were brought off by Col. Francis in good order; and the regiments which had preceded him, were soon recovered from their confusion. When the troops arrived at Hubbardton, they were halted for nearly two hours. Here the rear-guard was put under the command of Col. Seth Warner, with orders to follow the army, as soon as those, who had been left behind, came up, and to halt about a mile and a half in the rear of the main body. St. Clair then proceeded to Castleton, about six miles further, leaving Warner, with the rear-guard and stragglers, at Hubbardton."

* * * * * *

"The retreat from Ticonderoga was very disastrous to the Americans. Their cannon, amounting to 128 pieces,—their shipping and batteaux, and their provisions, stores and magazines, fell into the hands of the enemy. By this event, Burgoyne obtained no less than 1,748 barrels of flour, and more than 70 tons of salt provisions; and, in addition to these, a large drove of cattle, which had arrived in the American camp a few days previous to their retreat, fell into his hands."

Thompson's Vermont, Part 2, pp. 41–43.

See also

Williams' Hist. Vermont, Vol. 2. pp. 101–109.

(ɛ) "The retreat of the Americans from Ticonderoga was no sooner perceived by the British than an eager pursuit was begun by General Fraser with the light troops, who was soon followed by General Riedesel with the greater part of the Brunswick regiments. Fraser continued the pursuit during the day, and having learned that the rear of the American army was not far off, ordered his men to lie that night upon their arms. Early on the morning of the 7th he renewed the pursuit, and about 7 o'clock, commenced an attack upon the Americans under Warner. Warner's force consisted of his own regiment, and the regiments of Cols. Francis and Hale. Hale, fearful of the result, retired with his regiment, leaving Warner and Francis, with only seven or eight hundred men, to dispute the progress of the enemy.

"The conflict was fierce and bloody. Francis fell at the head of his regiment, fighting with great resolution and bravery. Warner, well supported by his officers and men, charged the enemy with such impetuosity that they were thrown into disorder, and at first gave way. They, however, soon recovered, formed anew, and advanced upon the Americans, who, in their turn, fell back. At this critical moment, a re-enforcement under Gen. Riedesel arrived, which was immediately led into action, and the fortune of the day was soon decided. The Americans, overpowered by numbers, and exhausted by fatigue, fled from the field in every direction.

"The loss of the Americans in this encounter was very considerable. Hale was overtaken by a party of the British, and surrendered himself, and a number of his men, prisoners of war. The whole American loss in killed, wounded and prisoners, was 324, of whom about 30 were killed. The loss of the enemy in killed and wounded, was 183.

"Gen. St. Clair, with the main body of the American army, was at Castleton, only six miles distant, during this engagement, but sent no assistance to Warner. After the battle, Warner, with his usual perseverance and intrepidity, collected his scattered troops and conducted them safely to Fort Edward, to which place St. Clair had retired with the army. While Gens. Fraser and Riedesel were pursuing the Americans by land, General Burgoyne himself conducted the pursuit by water. The boom and bridge between Ticonderoga and Mount Independence not being completed, were soon cut through, and by nine o'clock in the morning of the

6th the British frigates and gun-boats had passed the works. Several regiments were immediately embarked on board the boats, and the chase commenced. By three in the afternoon the foremost boats overtook and attacked the American gallies near Skenesborough, (now Whitehall,) and upon the approach of the frigates, the Americans abandoned their gallies, blew up three of them, and escaped to the shore. The other two fell into the hands of the British.

"As the American force was not sufficient to make an effectual stand at Skenesborough, they set fire to the works, mills and batteaux, and retreated up Wood Creek to Fort Ann. Being pursued by the ninth British regiment under Colonel Hill, the Americans turned upon him and gave him battle with such a spirit as to cause him to retire to the top of a hill, where he would have been soon overpowered, had not a re-enforcement come at that critical moment to his assistance. The Americans, upon this, relinquished the attack, and having set fire to Fort Ann, retreated to Fort Edward and joined the main army under Schuyler."

*   *   *   *   *   *

" After St. Clair had joined Gen. Schuyler at Fort Edward, and all the scattered troops had come in, the whole American force at that place did not exceed 4,400 men. Sensible that, with this force, it would be impossible to make an effectual stand, it became the chief object of the American generals to impede as much as possible the progress of the enemy by cutting down trees, blocking up the roads, and destroying the bridges.

"The works at Fort Edward being in no condition to afford protection to the American army, Gen. Schuyler abandoned them on the 22d of July, and retired with his whole force to Moses Creek, a position on the Hudson, about four miles below Fort Edward. At this place the hills approach very near the river on both sides, and this was selected as a favorable position to make a stand and dispute the progress of the enemy. But the army was found to be so much reduced by defeat and desertion, and the dissatisfaction to the American cause was found to be so general in this section of the country, that it was judged best to retire to Saratoga, and subsequently to Stillwater, at which place the army arrived on the 1st day of August."

Thompson's Vermont, Part 2, pp. 42, 43.
See also

Williams' Hist. Vermont, Vol. 2, pp. 105–107.
Gordon's American War, Vol. 2, pp. 483, 484.
Allen's American Rev., Vol. 2, pp. 31–33.
Thacher's Journal, Ed. of 1827, pp. 83–86.
Stone's Hist. of Beverly, pp. 73–79.
Trial of Gen. St. Clair.

The following account we take from one of the newspapers of the day:

"*July* 17.—By an express from the northward we learn that the American forces, under the command of General St. Clair, abandoned Fort Ticonderoga and the adjoining lines, on the morning of the 6th instant, and are now encamped in the vicinity of Moses Creek. A letter from an officer at that place, written this day, gives the following account of the retreat and its consequences:—The retreat from Ticonderoga will be a matter of speculation in the country, and the accounts different and confused, a true state of facts will therefore be very satisfactory without doubt.

"We were deceived with respect to the strength of the enemy, and our own reinforcements. The enemy have practised a piece of finesse which has too well answered their purpose; they have so conducted that all hands in the United States believed they had drawn their force from Canada to the southward, and designed only to garrison their posts in the northern world; the consequence of this belief has been the ordering eight regiments, destined for Ticonderoga and its environs, to Peekskill, and little attention has been paid to this department. The enemy's condition in Canada has been represented as miserable, confused, scattered and sickly; this has been the general opinion in camp and country, and our situation has been thought perfectly safe.

"Our force consisted of about four thousand, including the corps of artillery, and artificers who were not armed, a considerable part of which were militia; we could bring about three thousand fit for duty into the field. General Burgoyne came against us with about eight thousand healthy, spirited troops, with a lake force consisting of three fifty-gun ships, a thunder mounting eighteen brass twenty-four pounders, two thirteen-inch mortars, a number of howitz, several sloops, gun-boats, &c., &c.

"Their strength being so very superior to ours, obliged us to tamely sit still and see them erect batteries all around us, without hazarding a sally. Two batteries were erected in front of our lines, on higher ground than ours; within half a mile on our left they had taken post on a very high hill overlooking all our works; our right would have been commanded by their shipping and the batteries they had erected on the other side of the lake. Our lines at Ticonderoga would have been of no service, and we must have inevitably abandoned them in a few days after their batteries opened, which would have been the next morning; we then should have been necessitated to retire to Fort Independence, the consequence of which, I conceive, would have been much worse than the mode adopted; for the moment we had left Ticonderoga fort, they could send their shipping by us, and prevent our communication with Skenesborough; then the only avenue to and from Fort Independence would have been by a narrow neck of land leading from the mount to the Grants. To this neck they had almost cut a road; a day more would have completed it. A few troops stationed at Ticonderoga, would have prevented our communication with Lake George, as our own works would have been against us. Their shipping would have destroyed our connection with Skenesborough, and their main body might have been placed on this neck of land, which, by a few works, might have prevented all supplies and reinforcements; we might have stayed at the mount as long as our provisions would have supported us; we had flour for thirty days, and meat sufficient only for a week. Under these circumstances General St. Clair, on the sixth instant, called a council of war, and an evacuation was unanimously agreed upon as the only means of saving the army from captivity.

"It was necessary also that our retreat should be precipitate, as the communication was almost cut off, and they would soon be apprised of our designs. It was therefore determined to send the baggage and sick in boats to Skenesborough, and for the army to march by land from the mount to that place, being forty miles. At the dawn of day we left Fort Independence, and I cannot say the march was conducted with the greatest regularity; the front, which was the main body, marched thirty miles to a place called Castleton, about twelve miles from Skenesborough; the militia halted three miles in the rear of the front, and the rear guard, commanded by Colonel Francis, being joined by Colonels Warner and Hale, halted at Hubbardton, about a mile and a half in the rear of the militia. As the march was severe, the feeble of the army had fallen in the rear, and tarried at Hubbardton with the rear-guard. This body in rear might consist of near a thousand men. Before I proceed further, it may be necessary to give you the enemy's dispositions after they were advised of our retreat: A large body, at least two thousand, were detached to pursue our main body and harass our rear; all the gun-boats and some of their shipping were sent after our baggage, came up with it at Skenesborough and took it. The ninth regiment, commanded by Lieutenant-Colonel Hills, was ordered to run down South Bay, and land

and march on a by-road to Fort Ann, and take that before our troops could reach it ; the remainder of the army went on to Skenesborough, except a garrison at Ticonderoga.

" The body of the enemy sent to harass our rear, came up with it the next morning at Hubbardton, which was then commanded by Colonel Warner ; by the exertions of the officers, our little army formed and gave them battle, which continued about twenty-five minutes very severe, when our party were overpowered with numbers and gave way. The loss on both sides was considerable ; as our people took to the woods and are daily coming in, it is impossible to ascertain our loss. Colonel Francis, a worthy, brave officer, after signalizing himself, was shot through, and expired instantly ; Colonel Hale is missing. It is natural to ask, why was not Colonel Warner reinforced ? Let me tell you ; orders were sent to Colonel ——, who commanded the militia, to go to the assistance of the rear-guard, but before they arrived, the action was over and our people dispersed. Our main body being now twelve miles from Skenesborough, and hearing that a large body of the enemy were arrived there, and knowing that a large body were in our rear, the general imagined if we pursued our route, that we must engage both in front and rear under great disadvantage ; and to pursue his plan in first retreating, which was to save the army, he thought prudent to file off to the left, and before we reached Hudson River, we marched one hundred and fifty miles ; in this march we picked up about thirty prisoners, part British, part Waldeckers, and part Canadians. The party of our men who were at Skenesborough, retreated to Fort Ann; they were twice attacked by the ninth regiment, and both times repulsed them. They took a Captain Montgomery and a doctor, and would probably have taken the whole regiment had their ammunition held out. This is a candid statement of facts, and for this conduct we are told our country calls us either knaves or cowards; I conceive they ought to be grateful to our general, for had we stayed, we very certainly should have been taken, and then no troops could have stood between the enemy and the country. Our affairs now are not desperate in this quarter, as they would certainly have been; we have destroyed Fort George and its appendages, and shall soon be able, I hope, to make head against our enemies, as we are gathering strength and re-collecting ourselves."

Pennsylvania Evening Post, August 9th, 1777.

(0) OTTER CREEK, called by the French *la Rivière aux Loutres*, the River of Otters, is the longest stream of water in Vermont. It rises in Bennington Co., in the W. N. W. part of the State, and flowing in a N. N. W. course through Rutland Co., falls into Lake Champlain in Addison Co. In its course it receives about fifteen small tributary streams. Otter Creek, above Middlebury, is a very still stream, and its waters deep, affording very few mill privileges. From Middlebury to Pittsford, a distance of twenty-five miles, it is unavigable for boats. At Middlebury, Weybridge, and Vergennes, there are

falls in the creek which afford excellent sites for mills, and on which are some of the finest manufacturing establishments in the State. From Vergennes to the mouth, a distance of eight miles, the creek is navigable for the largest vessels on the lake. The whole length of the creek is about ninety miles, and it waters about nine hundred square miles.

(10) The HESSIANS were soldiers hired by Great Britain of some of the petty rulers of Germany, but from the circumstance of the greater number being derived from the principality of Hessen Cassel, they obtained the technical name by which they are now known, and which in course of time has become a term for mercenary troops generally. They were bought for a stipulated sum paid on account of each man on enlistment in the British army, while additional amounts became payable in the event of certain contingencies, such as wounds and death. The following table exhibits the quota obtained from the respective rulers, as well as the amount received by each :

Prince.	Number of men furnished.	Number lost.	Amounts received.
BRUNSWICK	5.723	3,015	£780,000
HESSEN CASSEL	16,992	6.500	2,600,000
HESSEN HANAU	2,422	981	335,150
ANSPACH	1,644	461	305,400
WALDECK	1,225	720	122.670
ANHALT	1.160	176	535,500
Total	29.166	11,853	4,678,620
HANOVER received			448,000
Total amount received			£ 5,126,620

Many of the troops were temporary sojourners in the principalities, and were secured by kidnapping, a mode which was practiced to a great extent. As this device relieved the citizens of Cassel from the evils of compulsory military service, it met with little or no opposition from them, and every traveler, therefore, had to depend chiefly on himself for safety. The necessary consequence of such a mode of recruiting was a great number of desertions, and to such an extent did these prevail, that from the regiment of Anhalt alone, one hundred and forty men deserted in one day, and on the next, their example was followed by an officer and fifty men. The Hessians arrived in America in 1776, and were first employed against the Americans in the battle of Long Island. They were subsequently engaged at Trenton, Princeton, Saratoga, and elsewhere. They were generally fine, hearty-looking men; wore large knapsacks on their backs, and spatter-dashes on their legs. A member of one of these regiments, says Dunlap, (*Hist. Amer. Theatre, Am. Ed.*, p. 45,) "with his towering brass-fronted cap, mustacios coloured with the same material that coloured his shoes, his hair plastered with tallow and flour, and tightly drawn into a long appendage reaching from the back of the head to his waist, his blue uniform almost covered by the broad belts sustaining his cartouch-box, his brass-hilted sword, and his bayonet; a yellow waistcoat with flaps, and yellow breeches were met at the knee by black gaiters, and thus heavily equipped, he stood an automaton, and received the command or cane of the officer who inspected him." The cavalry were mounted on gay ponies, much decorated with leather trappings. The accoutrements of themselves and their horses were heavy in the extreme. At the termination of the war, many of the Hessians settled down in America, and some of them became good and enterprising farmers and citizens.

(11) HUBBARDTON, a township in Rutland Co., Vermont, fifty miles N. of Bennington, and forty-six miles S. S. W. of Montpelier. It derived its name from Thomas Hubbard, who was a large proprietor. The settlement was commenced in the spring of 1774 by Uriah Hickok and William Trowbridge, who came with their families from Norfolk, Conn. Elizabeth, daughter of Mrs. Hickok, was born August 1st, 1774, and died in September, 1776. This was the first birth and the first death in the town. The first barn was built in 1785, and the first house in 1787. The first settlers of the town suffered very severely from the Indians and tories. There were but nine families in the town when the American army, under Gen. St. Clair, evacuated Ticonderoga, July 6, 1777. In 1810 the population was 642, and in 1860 it numbered 606.

(12) WHITE HALL, formerly called Skenesborough, a postvillage in Washington Co., N. Y., was organized in 1788. It is beautifully situated in White Hall township, at the head of the southern extremity of Lake Champlain, and on the Saratoga and Washington Railroad, seventy-seven miles N. by

E. of Albany. The Champlain canal terminates here, con-
necting the village with Troy. "The Indian name of the
town was '*Kah-cho-quah-na*,' the place where dip-fish." It
was formerly called Skenesborough from Maj. Philip Skene,
a royalist who resided here previous to the Revolution. The
pass at this place was seized by a detachment of volunteers
from Connecticut in May, 1775. Major Skene and his family,
with a number of soldiers, and several small pieces of cannon,
were taken. When Ticonderoga was abandoned on the
approach of Gen. Burgoyne, the public stores were embarked
on board of two hundred batteaux, and sent up the lake to
Skenesborough, under a convoy of five galleys. They were
pursued by a British brigade of gun-boats, and overtaken at
Skenesborough. Two of the galleys were taken, and the
other three blown up. The Americans being unable to make
an efficient stand, set fire to the works, fort, mills, batteaux,
and escaped as they could to Fort Ann. Skenesborough was
occupied by Burgoyne as his head-quarters for a considerable
time, while his troops were clearing a road to Fort Edward.
On the heights, overlooking the harbor, are the remains of a
battery and block house. The town carries on an extensive
trade with Canada. In 1860 the population of the township
was 4,862; of the village, 4,000.

(13) JOHN FLETCHER, the father of our author, was born in
Concord, Mass., and came to New Ipswich in 1758. He was
a cooper by trade. He was killed in New Ipswich in 1763,

by the falling of a tree. The family were led to the spot
through the strange conduct of their cat. The maiden name
of John Fletcher's wife was Elizabeth Foster. She was the
daughter of Abijah Foster, a farmer by occupation, and one
of the first settlers of New Ipswich. This lady was the first
female born in the place. She was born in the year 1741,
was married to John Fletcher in 1759, and died in the
year 1800.

(14) LUDLOW, a post village and township in Windsor Co.,
Vt., on a tributary of the Connecticut river, and on the Rutland and Burlington Railroad, about sixty-one miles S. of
Montpelier. In 1784–5, Josiah and Jesse Fletcher, Simeon
Reed, and James Whitney, all from Massachusetts, moved to
within the limits of the town, and began their clearings upon
the alluvial flats bordering upon Black River. Ludlow has
churches of three denominations, and considerable manufac-
tories of cassimeres, machinery and combs. The population
in 1860 was 1,568.

(15) NEW MARLBOROUGH, a post township in Berkshire Co.,
Mass., about 130 miles W. by S. of Boston. The first im-
provements in the town were made in 1739 by Benjamin
Wheeler, who came from Marlborough. During the severe
winter of 1739–40, he remained the only white inhabitant
in the town. The Indians, though in most respects friendly,
forbade him the use of his gun, lest he should kill the

deer, and thus withheld from him part of the means of his support. His nearest white neighbors were in Sheffield, ten miles distant. Some of these people came on snow-shoes to see him. In the town is a rock, judged to weigh thirty or forty tons, so equally balanced on another rock, that a man can move it with his finger. The population of the township in 1860 was 1,782.

(16) NEW-IPSWICH, a post-town in Hillsborough Co., N. H., on the west side of Souhegan river, upon the southern line of the State. It is distant fifty miles S. W. from Concord, and eighteen miles S. W. from Amherst. It was settled before 1749, by Reuben Kidder and others, and was incorporated Sept. 9th, 1762. The principal village is in the centre of the town, in a pleasant and fertile valley. Many of the dwelling-houses are of brick, and are elegant in appearance. The village contains a bank, a number of factories, and several cotton mills, the first of which was put in operation in 1803. The New-Ipswich Academy was incorporated June 18, 1789, has a fund of £1,000, and generally about forty or fifty students. New-Ipswich has produced many men, who have become eminent as patriots, merchants, and men of science. There were sixty-five men from this town in the battle of Bunker Hill. The population of the town in 1860 was 1,701.

(17) MAJOR-GEN. JOHN SULLIVAN was of Irish descent, and was born in Berwick, in the State of Maine, on the 17th day

of February, 1740. In his youth he worked upon a farm, but after arriving at maturity he studied law and established himself in practice in Durham, New Hampshire. His energy and industry soon rendered him a prominent man, and he was chosen a delegate to the first Congress. After his retirement from that body, he, with John Langdon, the Speaker of the Provincial Congress of New Hampshire, commanded a small force that seized Fort William and Mary, at Portsmouth, and carried off the cannon and powder. The next year he was again chosen a delegate to Congress, but being appointed by that body one of the eight brigadier-generals, in the new army, he soon proceeded to head-quarters at Cambridge. In the following year he was made a Major-General, and superseded Arnold in the command of the American army in Canada, but was soon driven out of that province. When Gen. Greene became ill on Long Island, Sullivan took command of his division, and in the battle of Brooklyn he was taken prisoner by the enemy. He was subsequently exchanged, and took command of Gen. Lee's division in New Jersey after the capture of that officer. In the autumn of 1777 he was engaged in the battles of Brandywine and Germantown, and in the winter following took command of the troops on Rhode Island. In August, 1778, he besieged Newport, then in the hands of the British, with the fullest confidence of success, but being abandoned by the French fleet under D'Estaing, who sailed to Boston, he was obliged to raise the siege. On the 29th an action took place with the pursuing enemy, who were repulsed with loss. On the following day, with much military skill, he passed over to the continent without the loss of baggage or life, and without the slightest suspicion on the part of the British of his movements. In the year 1779 he commanded an expedition against the Six Nations, and soon after his return, he resigned his commission. He was afterwards a member of Congress, and in 1786 became President of New Hampshire, which office he held for three years. While in this position he rendered important service in quelling the spirit of insurrection which exhibited itself at the time of the troubles in Massachusetts. In 1789 he was appointed District Judge of New Hampshire, a situation which he held at the time of his death. Gen. Sullivan was a man of short stature, but well formed and active. His complexion was dark, his nose prominent, his eyes black and piercing, and his face altogether agreeable. He was fond of display, but his deportment was dignified, commanding respect. He died in Durham, N. H., on the 23d day of January, 1795, in the 55th year of his age.

(18) The atrocities committed by the hostile Indians of the Six Nations, at Wyoming, Pa., and at several settlements in New York, determined Congress, in 1779, to send an army into the country inhabited by the savages, to retort upon them their own system of warfare. The force employed consisted of about five thousand men, and the command of the same was given to Gen. John Sullivan. The following is a particular account of the expedition:

" They were to make the attack by three different routes, by the way of the Susquehanna, the Mohawk and the Ohio rivers, while Washington, by a feint of entering Canada, should induce the British Governor-General to keep his forces at home. This plan was so far changed in its execution as to divide the whole force into two parts only ; the main body under Sullivan and the other under James Clinton, the Governor's brother. Sullivan reached Wyoming, on the Susquehanna, on the 21st July, having delayed his march, by waiting the result of extravagant demands which he continued to make for men, provisions, and equipments, and which Congress were not disposed to grant. The number of his troops, by the return of the 22d of July, amounted to no more than 2,312, rank and file, for the service of which, the Quarter-Master-General had supplied him with 1,400 horses. This force was more than three times greater than any probable number which the hostile Indians could bring against him, as the whole number of their warriors did not exceed 550, and to these were joined about 250 tories, the whole headed by Johnson, Butler and Brandt : yet Sullivan still demanded, and waited for more men. On the 21st of August, he was joined by General Clinton with 1,600 men, who had passed by the way of the Mohawk, without meeting opposition. It seemed to be the infatuated determination of General Sullivan to do everything in this expedition, which could blast the laurels he had hitherto won. He lived, during the march, in every species of extravagance, was constantly complaining to Congress that he was not half supplied, and daily amused himself in unwarrantable remarks to his young officers respecting the imbecility of Congress and the board of war.

"The hostile Indians and tories before mentioned, to the number of about 800, were posted at Newtown, where they had constructed works of considerable strength, and where they had been long expecting the approach of Sullivan. At length, on the 29th of August, the General arrived. He had with him six light field pieces and two howitzers, and as if determined that his march should be no secret, a morning and evening gun were regularly fired during his whole route. He seemed to consider the enemy as already in his power, and made the most absurd boast of his intentions with regard to them. The assault·was commenced by firing his light field pieces against their works, while a detachment under General Poor were ordered to march a mile and a half around the mountain, in full view of the enemy, for the purpose of attacking them on their left flank. Thus put on their guard, they waited the approach of General Poor, and would probably have given him battle; but his firing being the signal of other movements by Sullivan, they suddenly abandoned their works, and took to flight. Nothing could have been more mortifying to General Sullivan than this escape of what he had deemed a certain prize. He remained in the fort until the 31st, and then marched for Catharine's Town on the Seneca Lake. His road lay through the most dangerous defiles, and a swamp of considerable extent, through which a deep creek flowed in so meandering a course, that it was necessary to ford it seven or eight times. He arrived at the entrance of this swamp late in the afternoon, and was strongly advised not to venture into it until the next morning; but he persisted, and a miracle only prevented his obstinacy from bringing destruction upon his men. Some of the defiles through which he had to pass, were so narrow and dangerous that a score or two of Indians might have successfully disputed the passage against any number of men. The night was exceedingly dark, the men wearied, scattered and broken, and ready to die rather than move on; but the Indian scouts who had been sent to watch them, having retired as soon as it was dark, under the full persuasion that no General in his senses would attempt such a road by night, the defiles were fortunately unguarded, and the General arrived with his wearied army about midnight at the town. Clinton had halted at the entrance of the swamp, and pursued his march the next day.

" Sullivan continued for more than a month in the Indian country, laying waste and destroying everything, after the manner of his savage enemy, and completing the destruction of his fame. He arrived about the middle of October at Easton, in Pennsylvania, having in the course of his expedition killed *eleven* Indians and destroyed eighteen or twenty towns! Of the 1,400 horses which he had taken with him, 300 only were brought back. His childish and absurd complaints had disgusted the Commander-in-Chief, as well as the board of war, and the ridiculous vanity displayed in his official account

of the expedition, rendered him the jest of the whole army.
He was not long able to bear this downfall of his pride and
consequence, and on the 9th of November, he solicited permission to resign, which Congress readily accorded."

Allen's Amer. Rev., *Vol.* 2, pp. 276–279.
See also
Gordon's Amer. War, *Vol.* 3, pp. 307–312.

The following extract gives some interesting particulars respecting
the condition of the Indian settlements :

" Many settlements in the form of towns ·were destroyed,
besides detached habitations. All their fields of corn, and
whatever was in a state of cultivation, underwent the same
fate. Scarce anything in the form of a house was left standing, nor was an Indian to be seen. To the surprise of the
Americans, they found the lands about the Indian towns well
cultivated, and their houses both large and commodious. The
quantity of corn destroyed was immense. Orchards in which
were several hundred fruit trees were cut down, and many of
them appeared to have been planted for a long series of years.
Their gardens, which were enriched with great quantities of
useful vegetables of different kinds, were laid waste. The
Americans were so full of resentment against the Indians, for
the many outrages they had suffered from them, and so bent
on making the expedition decisive, that the officers and
soldiers cheerfully agreed to remain till they had fully completed the destruction of the settlement. The supplies
obtained in the country, lessened the inconvenience of short

rations. The ears of corn were so remarkably large, that many of them measured twenty-two inches in length. Necessity suggested a novel expedient for pulverising the grains thereof. The soldiers perforated a few of their camp kettles with bayonets. The protrusions occasioned thereby formed a rough surface, and by rubbing the ears of corn thereon, a coarse meal was produced, which was easily converted into agreeable nourishment."

Ramsay's Amer. Rev., Vol. 2, pp. 191-192.

See also

Campbell's Tryon Co., pp. 149-166.
Life of Van Campen, pp. 134-179.
Goodwin's Cortland Co., pp. 51-67.
Simms' Schoharie Co., p. 295.
Stone's Life of Brandt, Vol. 2, pp. 1-41.

(19) TIOGA POINT, in Bradford County, Pennsylvania, at the confluence of the Tioga and Susquehanna rivers, in the northern part of the State, is noted in the annals of Indian warfare as the site of an ancient Indian town, and as a place of rendezvous for parties or armies passing up or down the two great streams. The "Castle" of the celebrated Catharine Montour, sometimes called Queen Esther, was located here. The village of Athens now occupies the place of Gen. Sullivan's encampment.

(20) On the evening of Sept. 12th, 1779, while the army of Gen. Sullivan was encamped near an Indian town, on what is now known as Henderson Flats, a party of about twenty-one men, under command of Lieut. Thomas Boyd, was detached from the rifle corps, and sent out

to reconnoitre the ground near the Genesee river, at a place now
called Williamsburgh, about seven miles distant from the place of
encampment. On their return to the main army, they were attacked
by an overwhelming body of savages and tories, and Boyd and a man
named Parker were taken prisoners, and subsequently put to death,
the former in the most horrible manner, after having his nails pulled
out, his nose and tongue cut off, and one of his eyes plucked out. The
remainder of the party were all killed, with the exception of one
Timothy Murphy, who succeeded in making his escape. Shortly after
this occurrence, the bodies of Boyd and his slaughtered companions
were recovered by the army, and interred at a place now known as
Groveland. Their remains lay here until the year 1841, when they
were removed to Rochester and deposited in the cemetery at Mount
Hope, with appropriate civil and military honors, and in the presence
of a vast concourse of spectators. The following is a particular
account of the engagement of Lieut. Boyd and his party with the
Indians, and of the cruelties subsequently practiced upon him:

"When the party arrived at Williamsburgh, they found
that the Indians had very recently left the place, as the fires
in their huts were still burning. The night was so far spent
when they got to the place of their destination, that the
gallant Boyd, considering the fatigue of his men, concluded to
remain quietly where he was, near the village, sleeping upon
their arms, till the next morning, and then to despatch two
messengers with a report to the camp. Accordingly, a little
before daybreak, he sent two men to the main body of the
army, with information that the enemy had not been discovered, but were supposed to be not far distant, from the
fires they found burning the evening before.

"After day-light, Lieut. Boyd and his men cautiously crept
from the place of their concealment, and upon getting a view
of the village, discovered two Indians lurking about the

settlement; one of whom was immediately shot and scalped by one of the riflemen, by the name of Murphy. Lieut. Boyd—supposing now that if there were Indians near they would be aroused by the report of the rifle, and possibly by a perception of what had just taken place, the scalping of the Indian—thought it most prudent to retire and make his best way back to the main army. They accordingly set out, and retraced the steps they had taken the evening before.

" On their arriving within about one mile and a half of the main army, they were surprised by the sudden appearance of a body of Indians, to the amount of five hundred, under the command of Brandt, and the same number of rangers, commanded by the infamous Butler, who had secreted themselves in a ravine of considerable extent, which lay across the track that Lieut. Boyd had pursued. These two leaders of the enemy had not lost sight of the American army since their appalling defeat at the Narrows above Newtown, though they had not shown themselves till now. With what dismay they must have witnessed the destruction of their towns and the fruits of their fields, that marked the progress of our army! They dare not, however, any more come in contact with the main army, whatever should be the consequence of their forbearance.

" Lieut. Boyd and his little heroic party, upon discovering the enemy, knowing that the only chance for their escape would be by breaking through their lines, an enterprise of most desperate undertaking, made the bold attempt. As extraordinary as it may seem, the first onset, though unsuccessful, was made without the loss of a man on the part of the heroic band, though several of the enemy were killed. Two attempts more were made, which were equally unsuccessful, and in which the whole party fell. except Lieut. Boyd and eight others. Boyd, and a soldier by the name of Parker, were taken prisoners on the spot ; a part of the remainder fled. and a part fell on the ground apparently dead, and were overlooked by the Indians, who were too much engaged in pursuing the fugitives to notice those who fell.

" When Lieut. Boyd found himself a prisoner, he solicited an interview with Brandt, preferring, it seems, to throw himself upon the clemency and fidelity of the savage leader of the enemy, rather than trust to his civilized colleague. The chief, who was at that moment near, immediately presented himself, when Lieut. Boyd, by one of those appeals and tokens which are known only by those who have been initiated and instructed in certain mysteries, and which never fail to bring succor to a distressed brother. addressed him as the only source from which he could expect respite from cruel punishment or death. The appeal was recognized, and Brandt immediately, and in the strongest language, assured him that his life should be spared.

" Boyd and his fellow-prisoner were conducted immediately by a party of the Indians to the Indian village, called Beardstown, after a distinguished chief of that name. on the west side of the Genesee river, and in what is now called Leicester.

After their arrival at Beardstown, Brandt, being called on
service which required a few hours' absence, left them in the
care of Col. Butler. The latter, as soon as Brandt had left
them, commenced an interrogation, to obtain from the
prisoners a statement of the number, situation and intentions
of the army under Sullivan ; and threatened them, in case
they hesitated or prevaricated in their answers, to deliver
them up immediately to be massacred by the Indians; who,
in Brandt's absence, and with the encouragement of their
more savage commander, Butler, were ready to commit the
greatest cruelties. Relying probably upon the promises which
Brandt had made them, and which he most likely intended to
fulfill, they refused to give Butler the desired information.
Upon this refusal, burning with revenge, Butler hastened to
put his threat into execution. He delivered them to some of
their most ferocious enemies, among which the Indian chief
Little Beard was distinguished for his inventive ferocity. In
this, that was about to take place, as well as in all the other
scenes of cruelty that were perpetrated in his town, Little
Beard was master of ceremonies. The stoutest heart quails
under the apprehension of immediate and certain torture and
death ; where, too, there is not an eye that pities, nor a heart
that feels. The suffering Lieut. was first stripped of his
clothing, and then tied to a sapling, when the Indians
menaced his life by throwing their tomahawks at the tree
directly over his head, brandishing their scalping knives
around him in the most frightful manner, and accompanying

their ceremonies with terrific shouts of joy. Having punished him sufficiently in this way, they made a small opening in his abdomen, took out an intestine, which they tied to a sapling, and then unbound him from the tree, and by scourges, drove him around it till he had drawn out the whole of his intestines. He was then beheaded, and his head was stuck upon a pole, with a dog's head just above it, and his body left unburied upon the ground.

"Thus perished Thomas Boyd, a young officer of heroic virtue, and of rising talents; and in a manner that will touch the sympathies of all who read the story of his death. His fellow-soldier, and fellow-sufferer, Parker, was obliged to witness this moving and tragical scene, and in full expectation of passing the same ordeal.

"According, however, to our information, in relation to the death of these two men, which has been obtained incidentally from the Indian account of it, corroborated by the discovery of the two bodies by the American army, Parker was only beheaded."

Wilkinson's Annals of Binghampton. pp. 34–38.
See also
   Stone's Life of Brandt. Vol. 2, pp. 29–33.
   Life of Jemison, pp. 121–122 and p. 291.
   Simms' Schoharie Co., pp. 312–13.
   Life of Van Campen, pp. 160–173.
   Notices of Sullivan's Campaign.

The following additional facts respecting Lieut. Boyd were obtained from Josias E. Vrooman, who witnessed the parting scene therein described:

"Lieut. Boyd was a native of Northumberland County,

Pennsylvania. He was about the usual height, and was a stout built, fine looking young man; being very sociable and agreeable in his manners, which had gained him many friends in Schoharie. While there, he paid his addresses to Miss Cornelia, a daughter of Bartholomew Becker, who gave birth to a daughter after his death, of which he was the reputed father. This child, named Catharine, grew up a very respectable woman, and afterwards became the wife of Martinus Vrooman. While the troops under Col. Butler were preparing to leave Schoharie, Miss Becker, in a state of mind bordering on phrensy, approached her lover, caught hold of his arm, and in tears besought him by the most earnest entreaties, to marry her before he left Schoharie. He endeavored to put her off with future promises, and to free himself from her grasp. She told him " if he went off without marrying her, *she hoped he would be cut to pieces by the Indians.*" In the midst of this unpleasant scene, Col. Butler rode up and reprimanded Boyd for his delay, as the troops were ready to march—and the latter, mortified at being seen by his commander, thus importuned by a girl, *drew his sword and threatened to stab her if she did not instantly leave him.* She did leave him, and anticipating future shame, called down the vengeance of heaven upon him. Her imprecation was answered, as has been seen, to the fullest extent : a fearful warning to those who trifle with woman's affections."

Simms' Hist. of Schoharie Co., p. 300.

(21) The following extract, from an English writer, gives one of the best descriptions which we have met with, of the personal appearance and character of the " Father of his country " :

*　　*　　*　　*　　*　　*

" General Washington is now in the forty-eighth year of his age. He is a tall, well-made man, rather large boned, and has a tolerably genteel address, his features are manly and bold, his eyes of a bluish cast, and very lively; his hair a deep brown, his face rather long, and marked with the small-pox ; his complexion sun-burnt, and without much color, and his countenance sensible, composed, and thoughtful. There is a remarkable air of dignity about him, with a striking degree of gracefulness; he has an excellent understanding, without much quickness; is strictly just, vigilant, and generous ; an affectionate husband, a faithful friend, a father to the deserving soldier, gentle in his manners, in temper rather reserved ; a total stranger to religious prejudices, which have so often excited Christians of one denomination to cut the throats of those of another. In his morals he is irreproachable, and was never known to exceed the bounds of the most rigid temperance. In a word, all his friends and acquaintances universally allow, that no man ever united in his own character a more perfect alliance of the virtues of the philosopher with the talents of a general. Candor, sincerity, affability, and simplicity, seem to be the striking features of his character, until an occasion offers of displaying the most determined bravery and independence of spirit."

*　　*　　*　　*　　*　　*

London Chronicle, July 22, 1780.

(₂₂) GILBERT MOTTIER, MARQUIS DE LA FAYETTE, was born in Chavaniac, iu the ancient province of Auvergne, in France, Sept. 6, 1757. He was descended from distinguished ancestors, and was the inheritor of a princely fortune. He was educated at Paris, and at the age of 17 married the Countess Anastasie de Noailles, by whom he received a large accession to his estate. In the year 1777, the most gloomy period of the American struggle, this young nobleman, then only 19 years of age, actuated by a love of liberty as pure as it was ardent, left the luxuries of the court, and the endearments of his young wife, and in opposition to the wishes of his friends and the orders of his sovereign, embarked for America, in a vessel fitted out by himself, to aid a people to whom he was bound by no tie of tongue or kindred, and who were then too poor to offer him even a transport to their shores. Upon his arrival in America, he offered himself to Congress as a volunteer, solicited permission to serve without pay, and raised and equipped a body of men at his own expense. In July he was appointed by Congress a Major-General, and in September he served as a volunteer at the battle of Brandywine, in which engagement he was severely wounded. After his recovery he joined Gen. Greene in New Jersey, and in the battle of Monmouth, in 1778, he rendered most important services, for which he received the thanks of Congress. He continued actively employed in different parts of the country until 1779, when he went to France, and after securing aid from that quarter, returned to America. He immediately resumed his command, and in the campaigns of 1780 and 1781, displayed the most consummate generalship. At the siege of Yorktown he shared in the dangers and honors of the day, and after the capitulation of Cornwallis, left again for France. He was about to return to America with a powerful fleet and army, when he received the glorious news of the overtures of peace. In 1784 he visited America, and after spending a few days at Mount Vernon, traveled through the principal cities of the Union, receiving everywhere the honors that were his due. After his return to France, he held a number of prominent positions, both civil and military. In the year 1824, he again visited America, where he was received with the most enthusiastic demonstrations of respect and affection. Congress made him a grant of 200,000 dollars and a township of land, and he was carried home in the frigate Brandywine, so named in honor of his bravery in that memorable battle. After his return to France he again engaged in public affairs, taking an active part in the revolution of 1830, at which time he became marshal of France.

"Gen. Lafayette was about six feet in stature. He was considered one of the finest looking men in the American army, notwithstanding his deep red hair, which then, as now, was rather in disrepute. His forehead was fine though receding—his eye clear hazel—his mouth and chin delicately formed and exhibiting beauty rather than strength. The expression of his countenance was strongly indicative of the generous and gallant spirit which animated him, mingled with something of the pride of conscious manliness. His mien was noble—his manners frank and amiable, and his movementslight and graceful. He wore his hair plain, and never complied so far with the fashion of the times as to wear powder."

After a long and eventful career, this devoted friend of Washington and America died at Paris, on the 20th day of May, 1834, in the 77th year of his age. Admired and honored in life, he died universally lamented, leaving behind him a name which the proudest monarch may envy and the most ambitious warrior well emulate—that of a disinterested, noble minded and consistent patriot. Dearly beloved as he was, his memory will ever be fresh in the heart of every true friend to his country.

.

(23) Ebenezer Fletcher, as we have before remarked, was married in the year 1786 to Miss Polly Cummings. The father of this lady, Mr. Samuel Cummings, was at that time a resident of New Ipswich, and owner of the mills at Mill Village. He carried on the mills successfully for a number of years, and then sold them out to Mr. Fletcher, who had learned the trade of him. Mr. Cummings subsequently moved to Cornish, N. H., and died there on the sixth day of June, 1796, at the age of seventy-eight years. Mr. Fletcher, by his first wife, who died on the 26th day of February, 1812, had six sons and six daughters, whose names and places of birth and death are as follows :

Born in New Ipswich, N.H.   Died.

1st. EBENEZER, Jr. .Oct. 9, 1782. .Nov. 14, 1834, in Corinth, N. H.
2d. CUMMINGS ....July 5, 1784. .July 22. 1837, " Enosburg, Vt.
3d. JOHN ....Aug. 14, 1786 July 10, 1842, " Ann Arbor, Mich.
4th. POLLY........Aug. 21, 1788. .Aug. 27, 1840, " Illinois.
5th. JOSEPH ......May 22, 1790. .Feb. 18, 1863, " Ashburnham, Mass.
6th. BETSEY ......Dec. 28, 1792. .May 5, 1842, " Boston, Mass.
7th. SALLY)   *Twins.* Feb. 6, 1794) July 17. 1854, " New Ipswich. N.H.
8th. MILLY)   ) " 11, 1794. "   "
9th. NANCY ....May 22, 1797....Still living "   "   "
10th. DEXTER ......Ap'l 19, 1799 ... "   "   " Mt. Vernon,   "
11th. SUKY.........May 30, 1801. .Aug. 13, 1803, " New Ipswich,   "
12th. ROBY ....June 16, 1803....Still living "   "   "

Mr. Fletcher's second wife was Mrs. Mary Foster, widow of Nathaniel Foster, and daughter of Asa Kendall. She had no children by Mr. Fletcher. By her first husband she had two sons and five daughters. She was a member of the Baptist church for many years, and sustained a good Christian character. She survived her husband, Mr. Fletcher, a number of years, and died in Winchendon, Mass., January 25th, 1851, at the age of 85 years.

FINIS